THE ART OF KUMOMI

Finding Meaning in Randomness

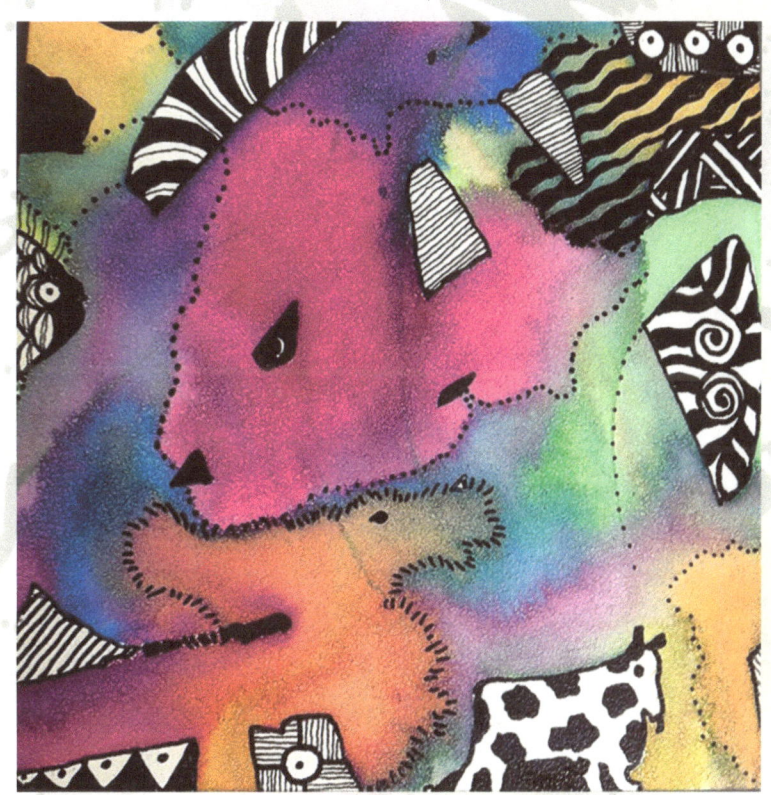

Karen Elaine

Copyright © 2015 Karen Elaine Parsons

ISBN-10: 1502328585   ISBN-13: 978-1502328588

CONTENTS

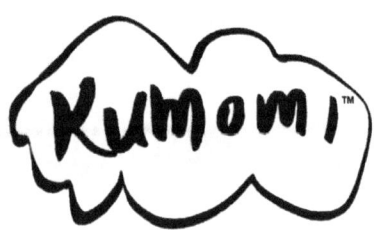

INTRODUCTION

The purpose in developing Kumomi was to have a simple creative process combining the randomness of spontaneous painting with the control of mindful drawing as a meditative art form.

I was intrigued by the idea meditative art but I found intricate patterns difficult to remember. Skill in art or having excellent dexterity is not necessarily a requirement to receive the benefits of Kumomi. The end result is not necessarily to create a masterpiece but to enjoy the creative process, relax the body and open the mind. If you practice Kumomi regularly you will very likely see improvements in your mental, physical and emotional well being.

Brilliant colors interacting with each other is the core of Kumomi followed by mindful drawing using a fine tipped pen. The process combines the joyful aspect of color with mindful drawing along with meditative music to achieve a goal of enhanced relaxation and creativity. The process is very simple and for those who already practice meditative art, Kumomi will be a great addition of color and spontaneity.

Kumomi, can be a pleasurable and relaxing experience for people of all ages and skill levels. Let go of perfectionism and preconceived ideas and play with joyful colors and lines. Be open to creative ideas and possibilities and most of all, enjoy the process.

Karen Elaine

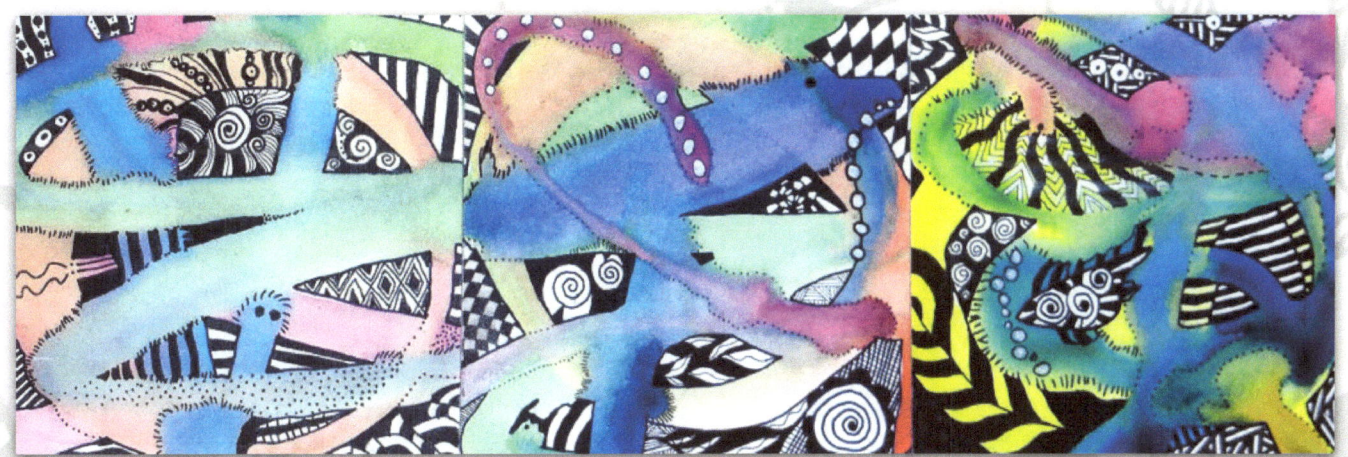

WHAT IS KUMOMI?

Kumomi is the combination of Japanese characters for *cloud* and to *see* so it essentially means *cloud gazing*.

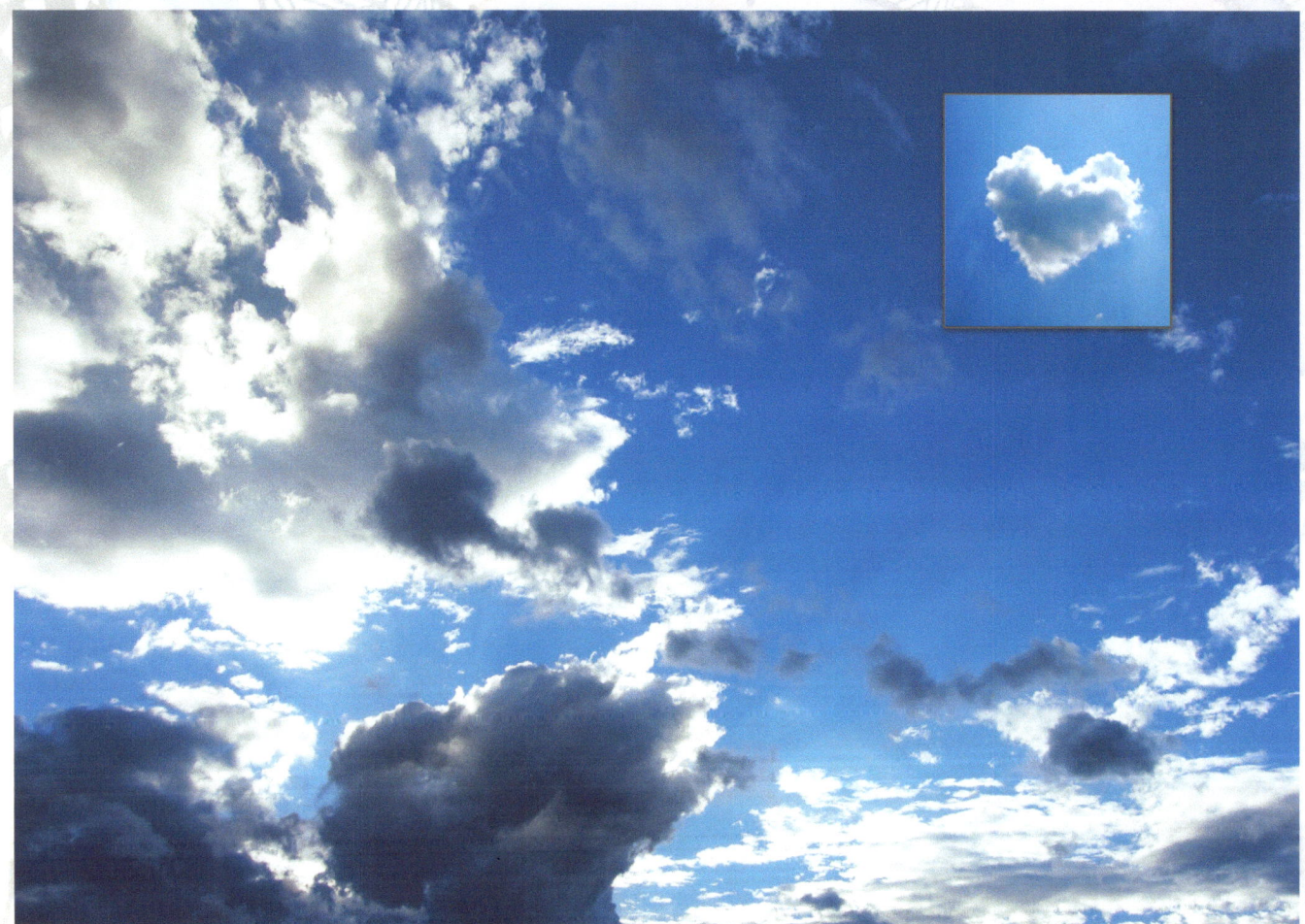

FINDING MEANING IN RANDOMNESS

Imagine watching puffy white clouds drift slowly across the blue sky changing shape as they go. You may see a duck, a heart, a boat, an angel or any number of things. This psychological phenomenon known as *pareidolia* causes human beings to seek something familiar in otherwise random shapes. It is the result of our brains trying make sense out of something that doesn't make sense at all. The Kumomi creative process brings the experience of cloud gazing and combines it with art and meditative music to invoke a merging of the senses for a mind expanding experience.

Music & Creativity

It is widely known that music enhances creativity and I believe calming music is an essential component to the Kumomi experience.

Music gives our brain an opportunity to practice abstract and creative thought. Research shows that listening to slow music enhances cognitive functions such as memory and concentration. It is also known to boost the immune system, lower blood pressure, relax muscles, regulate stress hormones, elevate mood and increase endurance.

Simply listening to music relaxes the body and stimulates the imagination. When you combine the activity of painting and drawing you are engaging yourself completely in the present moment which is a powerful form of meditation.

Choose any soothing, new age or classical music for your Kumomi practice. I discovered Liquid Mind Music several years ago during a very stressful time in my life and it helped me achieve a heightened state of relaxation more than any other meditation music I have listened to. Listen to different classical and contemporary composers and find meditative music that resonates with you. If you practice Kumomi in silence you will still receive the benefit of enhancing creativity and relaxation.

Most importantly, let go, relax and enjoy.

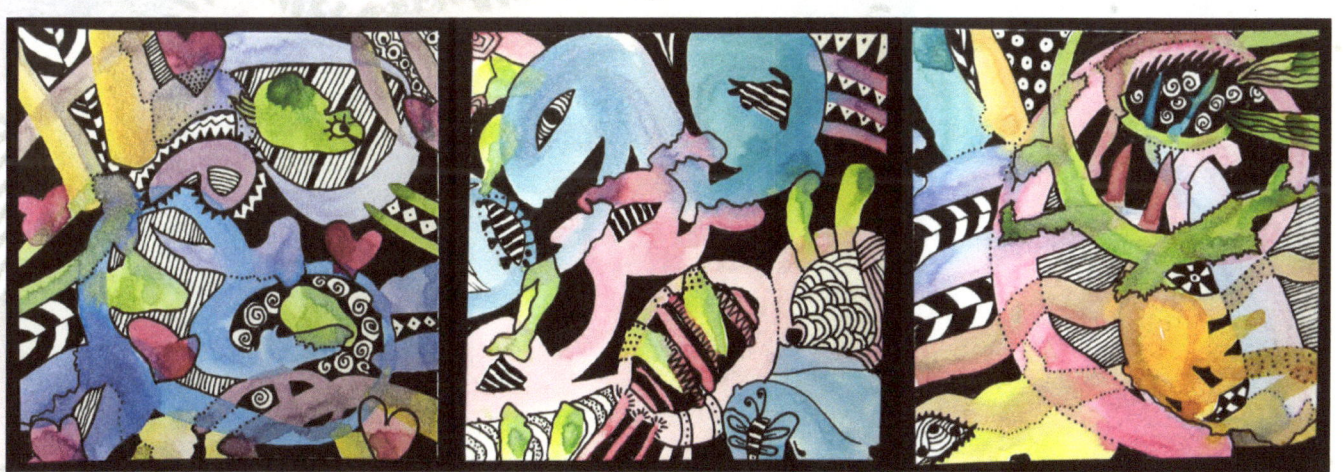

GATHERING SUPPLIES

While developing Kumomi I experimented with many types of paints, pens and surfaces. I achieve the most brilliant colors and dense black details with these specific products but you can successfully practice Kumomi with transparent watercolors, fluid acrylics, even food coloring and with art supplies you may already own.

Splash Ink magenta, blue and yellow

Large synthetic hair round watercolor brush

4" square smooth surface artist tiles or masonite

Black felt tipped pens in assorted sizes.

Opaque white pen or marker (optional)

Paper palette or plastic tray

Water & water container

Paper towels

A sheet of plain paper

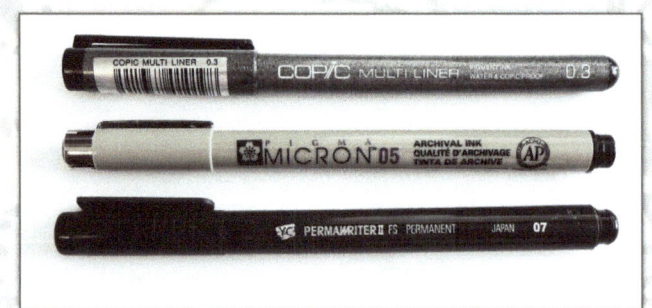

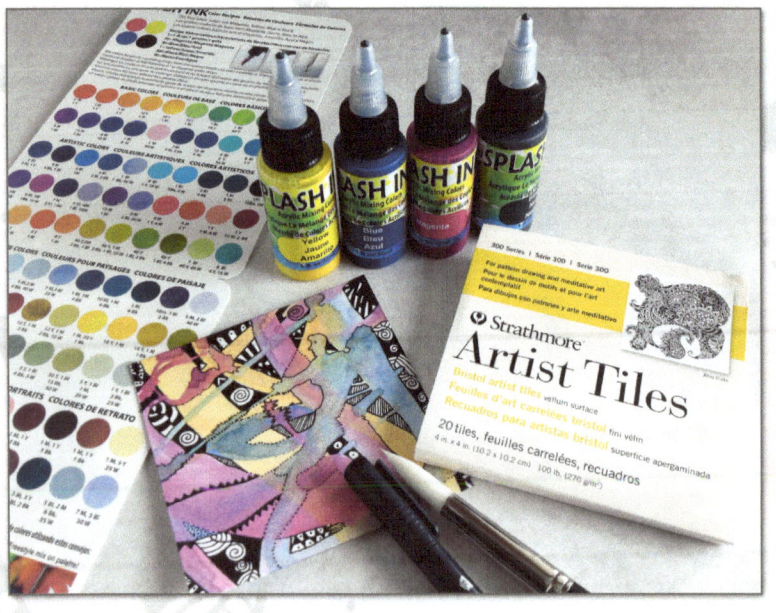

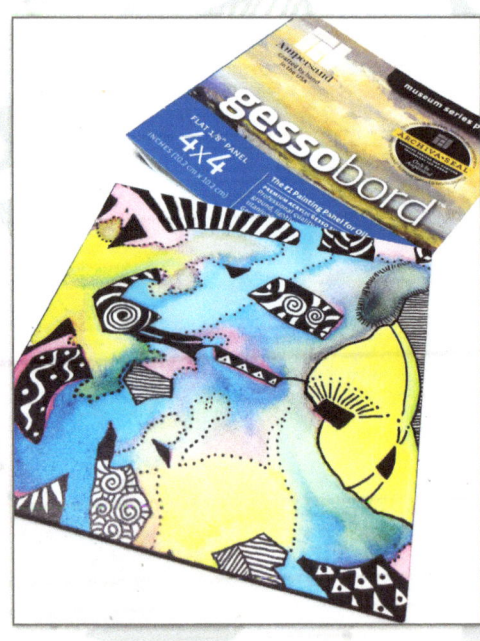

CREATING A SPACE

Set up a small area or workspace to practice Kumomi regularly. Very little space is needed but you will need to work in a well lit area and conducive to meditation away from distractions.

Find a basket or container to organize the supplies so they are ready when you are. Make sure the work area is free of clutter. Start the music, empty your mind and fill your water container with plenty of clean water. Sit in a comfortable chair and keep your back as straight as possible. Keep both feet on the ground and get into to the zone of meditation.

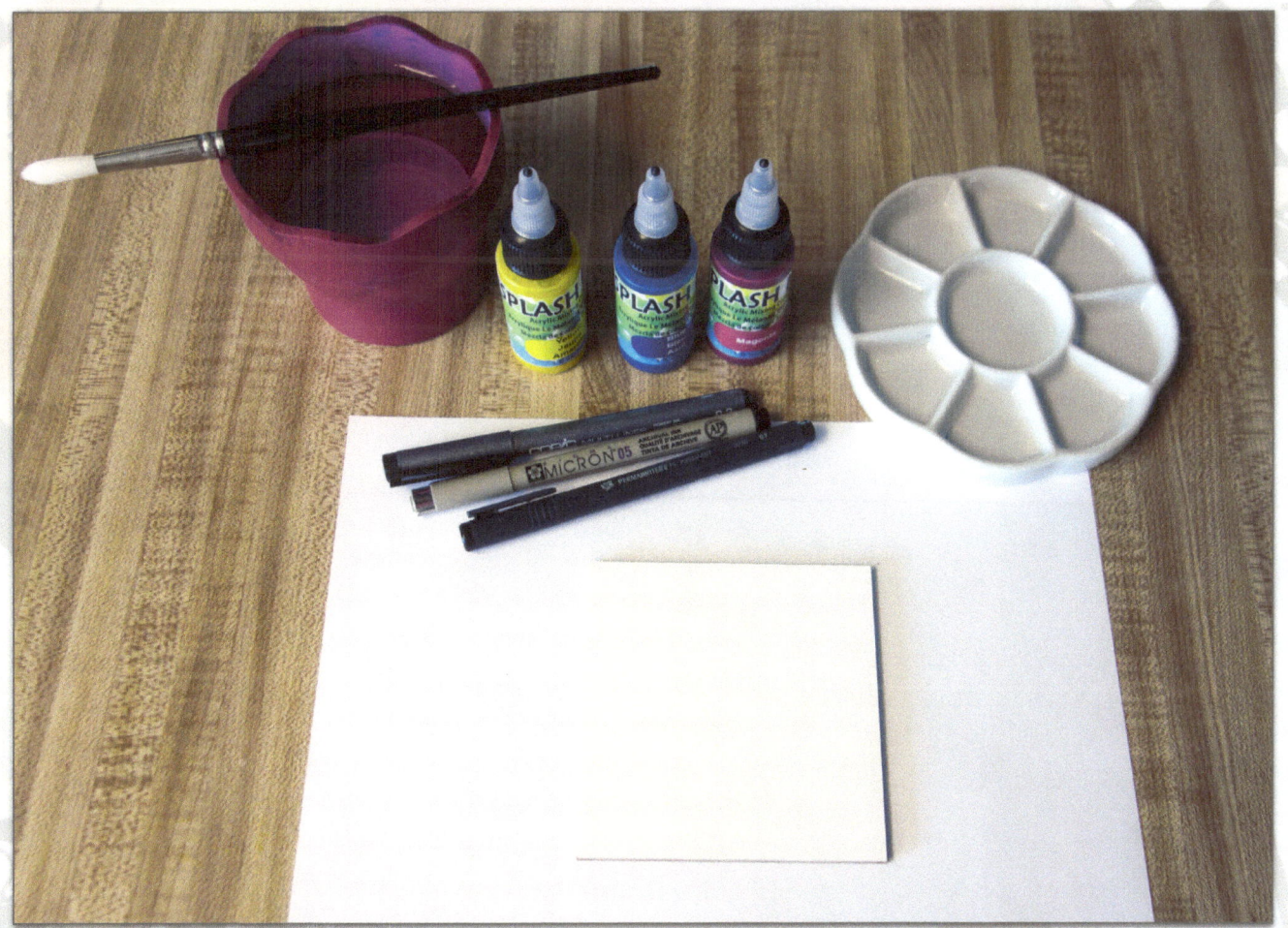

The kitchen table is a great place to practice Kumomi!

LET'S BEGIN!

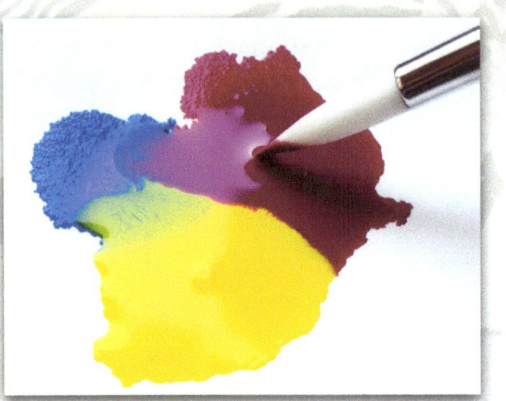

Squeeze several drops of magenta, blue and yellow Splash Ink, acrylics or watercolors onto a palette or a non porous mixing surface. Create saturated color combinations including variations of reds, purples, greens, oranges, golds and blues.

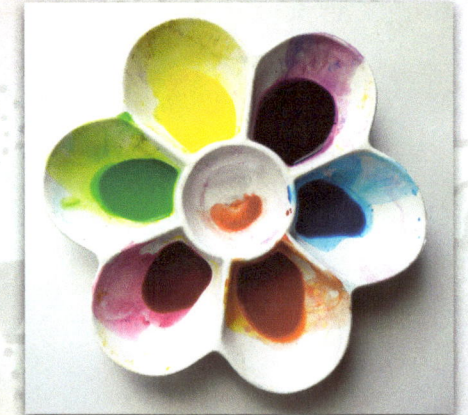

The preparation is just as important as the painting so take your time while mindfully creating new colors. Observe the mixing process and be sure to clean your brush in-between each color. Have an assortment of colors mixed on the palette or in a dish before you begin painting on the tiles.

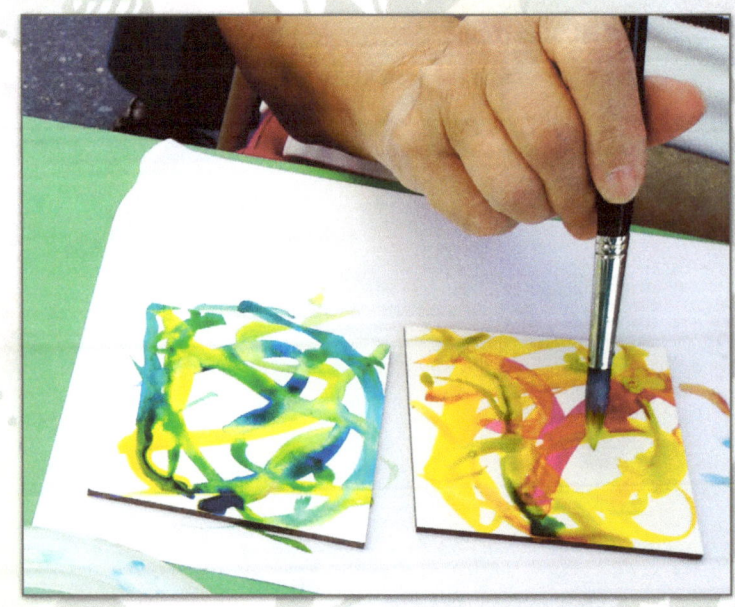

It is very important to use plenty of water as you paint.

The more water you use, the more interesting the effects will be. When working with watercolors, inks or fluid acrylics, water is the first ingredient so use in generous amounts.

Splash Ink colors are very concentrated so water is essential.

Paint spontaneously!

Place a 4″ paper or board tile onto a sheet of plain white office paper. The white paper is important because you will be extending your brush strokes off the tile and onto the paper. This will make a better composition and you won't confine the expressive strokes to the tile.

Pick up a generous amount of mixed colors with a brush and paint random strokes onto the tile going in different directions making sure the strokes extend beyond the tile onto the white paper underneath.

Change colors in-between each stroke or letter by rinsing them out in clean water. The colors will blend together when they touch each other on the tile as you will be working very quickly in this part of the process. Observe colors blending together making new colors right on the surface of the tile. For best results be sure to use a surface that will allow the colors to float and blend. If a color soaks in right away and looks grainy, the surface is too absorbent.

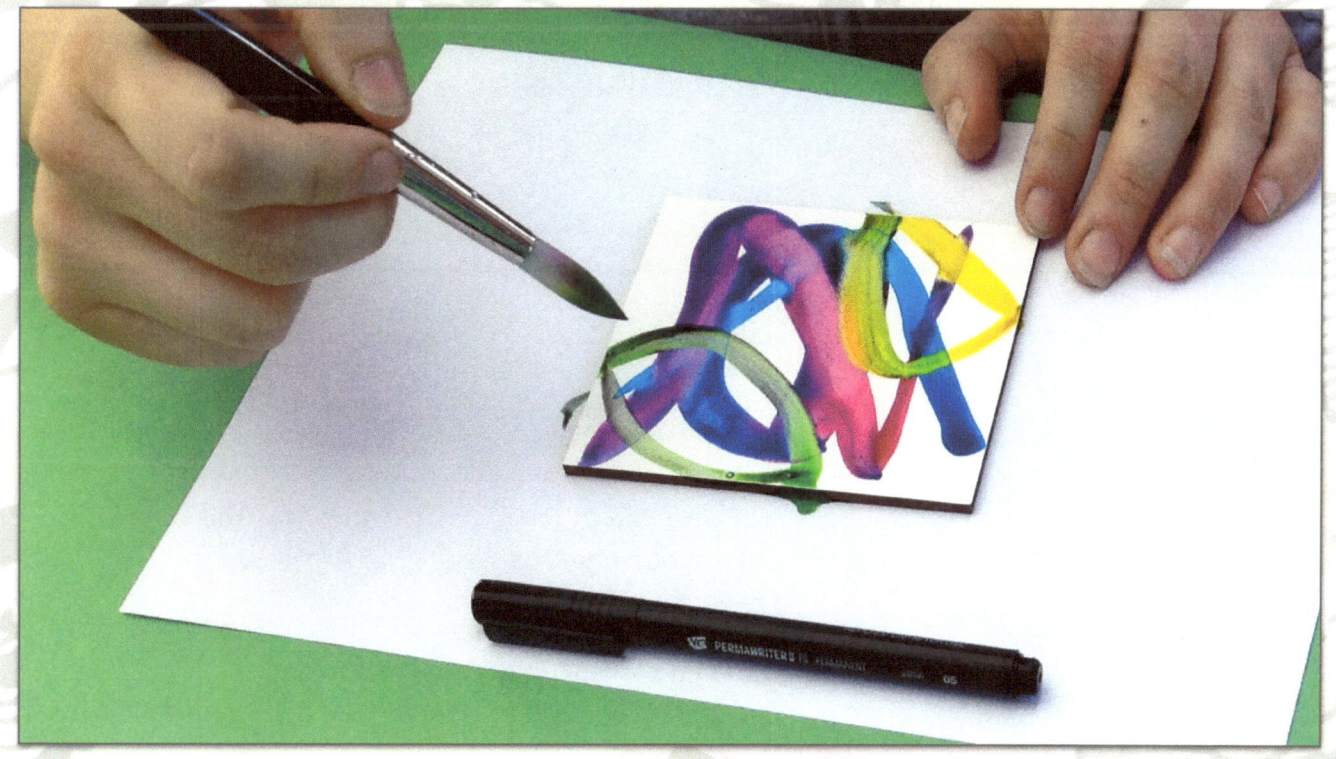

STATE YOUR INTENTION

Think of a word, someones name or an intention and write large expressive letters overlapping each other using your brush. The word will be unrecognizable but you will know it's meaning.

Change colors with every letter by cleaning your brush between each letter.

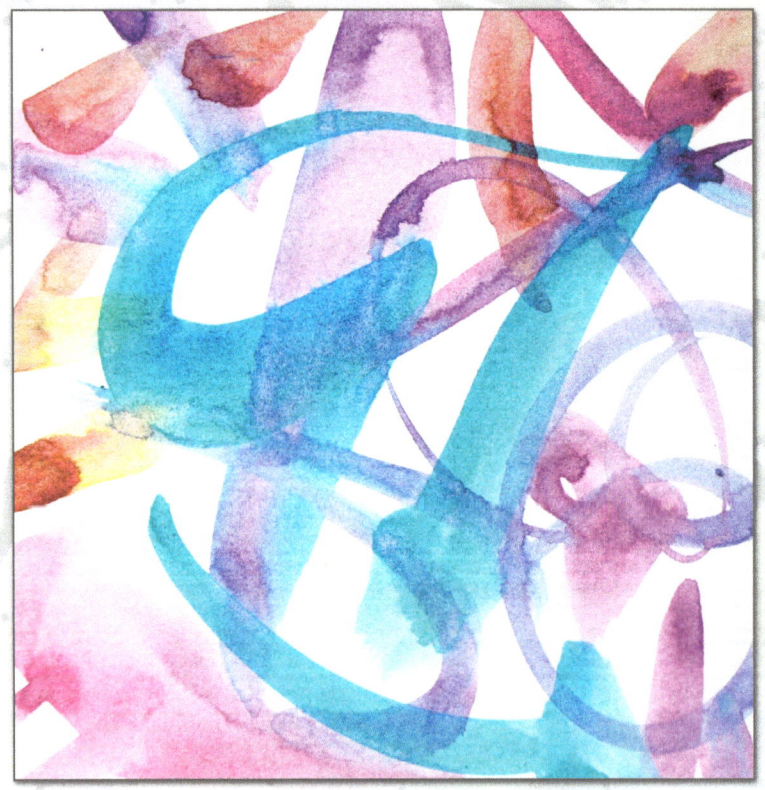

Make sure the strokes are wet, loose and large. Paint loosely with your arm and wrist, not restricted to your fingertips.

Leave some areas unpainted because the white space is as important as the painted areas. Paint several tiles at a time and set aside to dry completely.

FIND MEANING IN RANDOMNESS

Outline the areas in-between the painted edges and the white areas with the pen. Use a larger tip such as an .08 or .05 to make the lines. Go slowly and deliberately while going around every curve. Let let your mind go and relax. Take a moment after outlining the areas in between the colors and look for familiar objects in the shapes. If you don't see anything familiar, that's okay too. Set aside the tile to do some practice drawing.

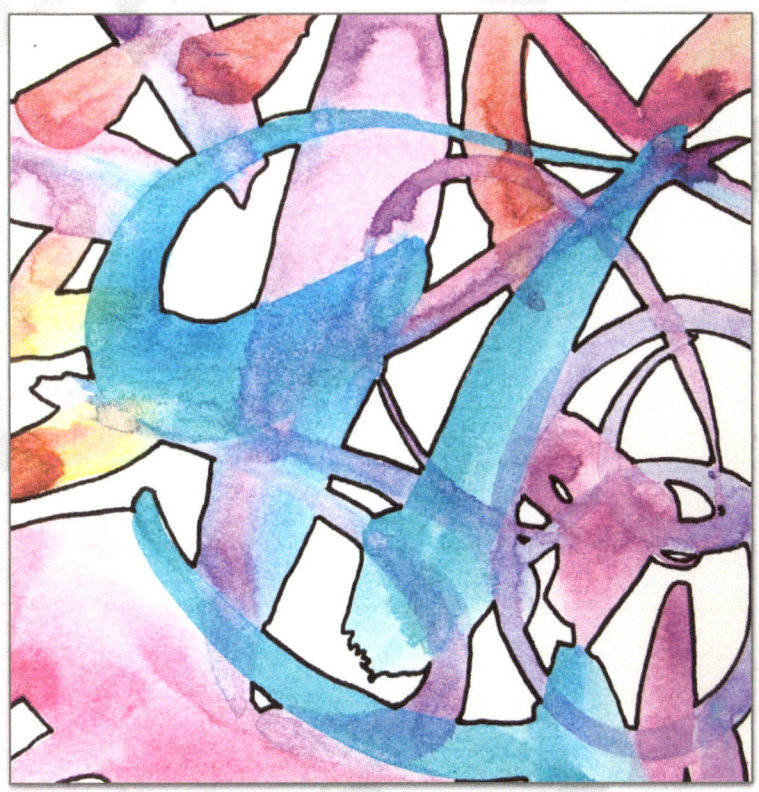

A NOTE ON PENS

Fine tipped pigmented pens are recommended for the paper tiles. Permanent (solvent based) pens are recommended for masonite or painted tiles because they dry faster and stick to slicker surfaces. Before drawing on the tile, make sure your pen makes a consistent, dense black line. To keep the pens from drying out prematurely, firmly replace the cap and store them in a zip-lock bag.

Practice mindful Drawing

On a separate sheet of paper, practice mindful drawing using a pen. Draw at least 10 small rectangles on the paper and draw inside the rectangles. Make spirals, hatch marks, zig-zags, dotted lines, dashed lines, loops and mazes inside the rectangles.
Draw on this page or make a copy of it to practice drawing.

Spirals	Hatch Marks	Curvy Dotted Lines	Curvy Dashed Lines

Spirals with Tails	Leaf Veins	Zig-Zags	Zig-Zags Crossed Out

Checker Board	Wavy Checker Board	Wavy Lines	Loops

Create Your Own!

This is my practice sheet to use as a reference. I used familiar shapes and images and made deliberate, controlled lines. The drawings don't have to be perfect and everyone will find their own style. Become accustomed to drawing slowly and mindfully.

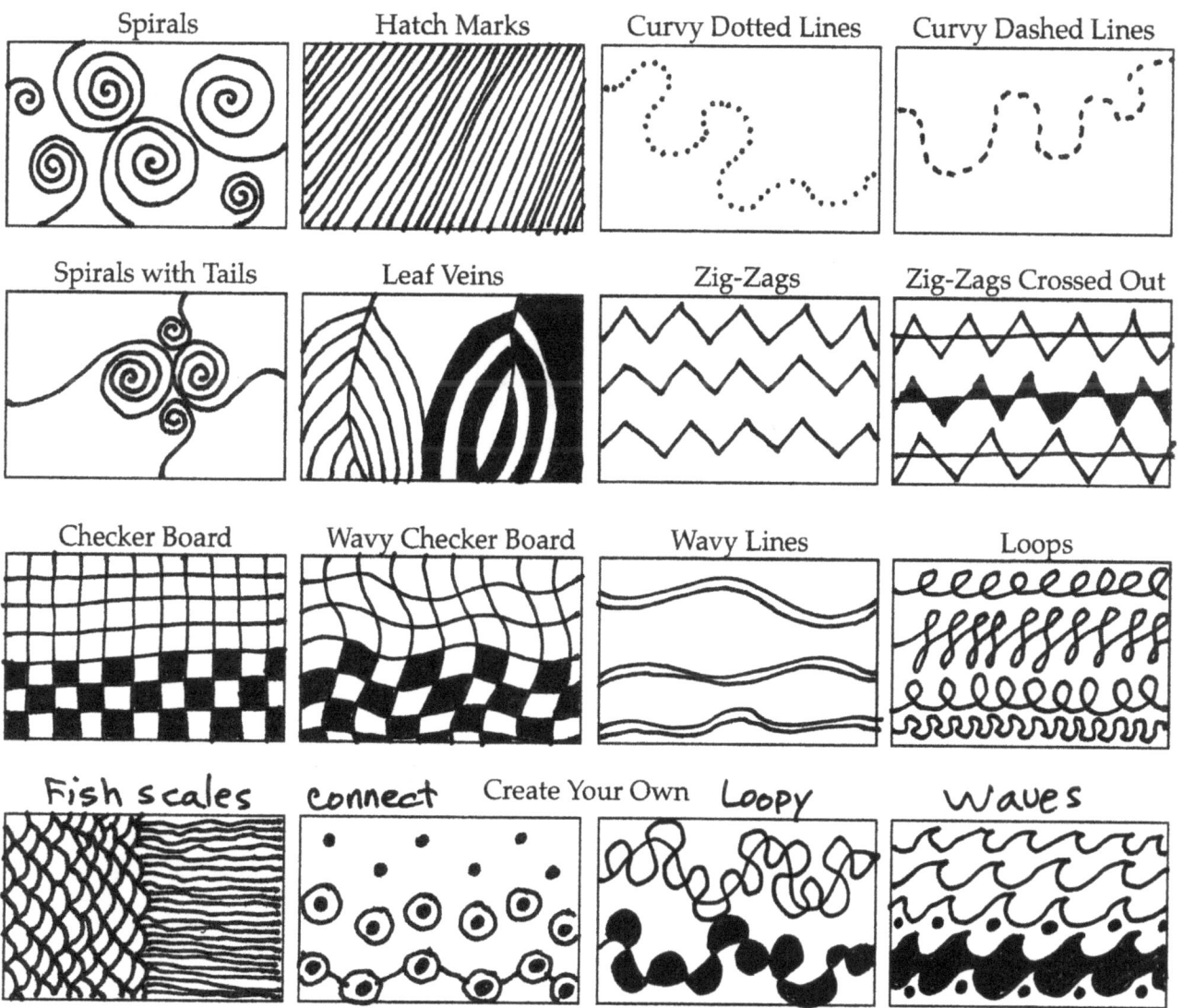

THE ESSENCE OF CLOUD GAZING

Draw dotted or dashed lines to bring out the edges of the strokes inside the colors. Bring out the familiar shapes if you see them. Draw an eye if you see a face and fins or scales if you see a sea creature emerge. This is where your creative mind will take over. Let your imagination soar as if you are looking into a sky filled with clouds. Draw slowly and mindfully. Bring out the shapes slowly with the pen and watch your drawing transform.

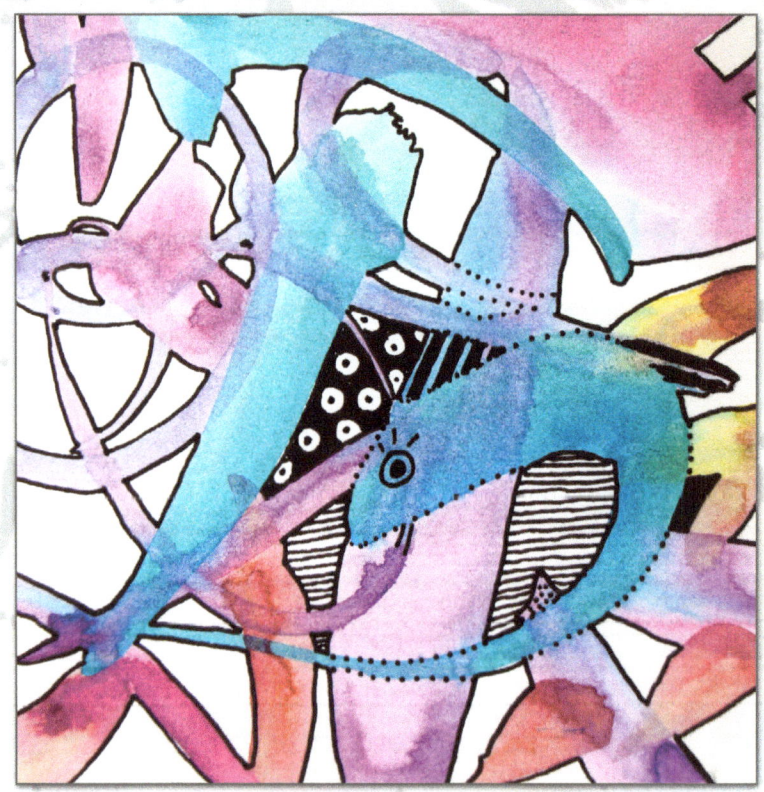

If you don't see a familiar shape, then draw an assortment of random patterns inside the lined areas. Make assorted hatch marks, swirls, checkerboards, organic shapes or learned patterns. Vary the width of the lines using different pen sizes.

There is no wrong way to do this! Everyone has uniquely beautiful way of expressing themselves and it's the process that has meaning, not necessarily the final product.

Continue to draw slowly and mindfully. Fill in areas with solid black for drama and contrast. The solid black areas will bring out the shapes even more. Take a moment and observe the work as it unfolds in front of you.

Stop drawing when you have covered the tiles leaving a balance of pattern, color and solid areas of black and white. Only you will know when it is finished.

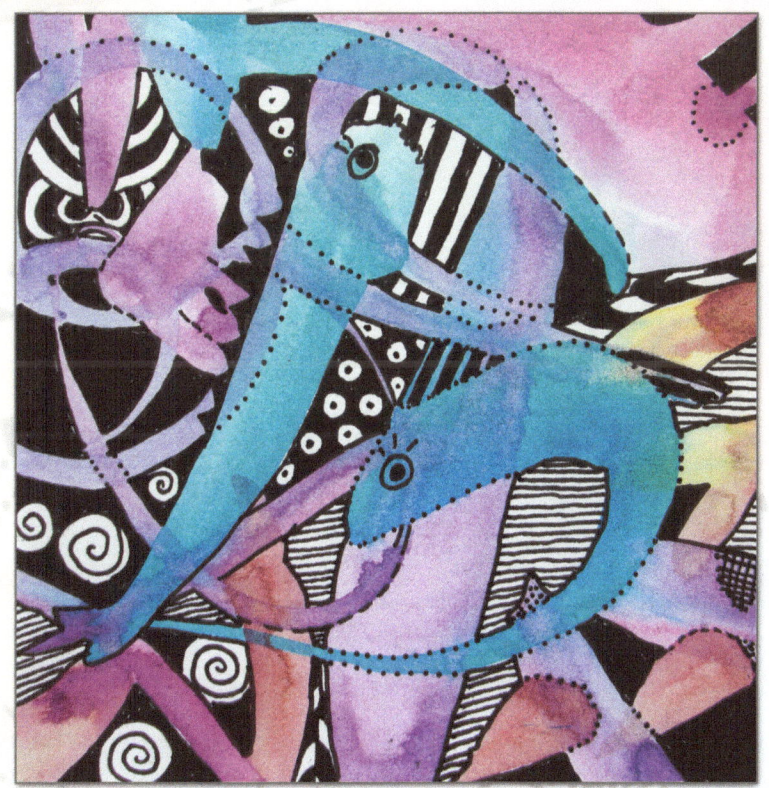

Record the date and write thoughts or feelings that Kumomi may have invoked on the back of the tile. Give it a title to represent the feelings or things it represents.

The Kumomi experience will follow you into your other work and you will see new creative opportunities you would have otherwise missed. Practicing Kumomi regularly will very likely expand your consciousness!

Kumomi on Paper

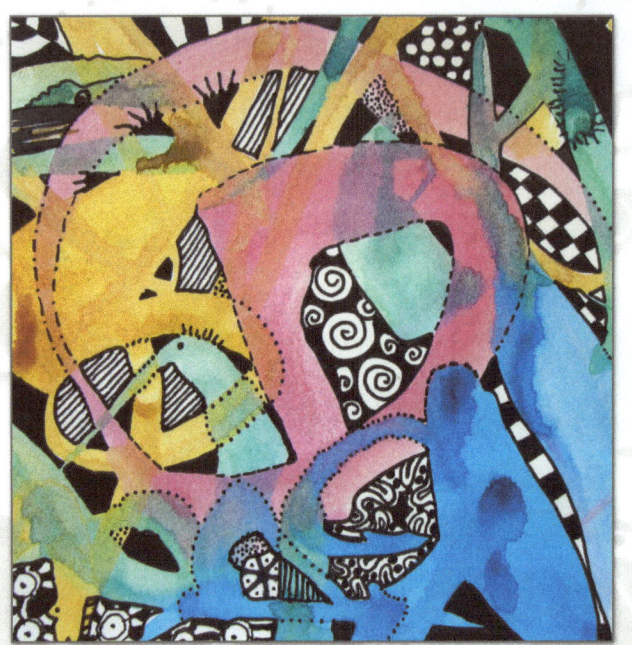
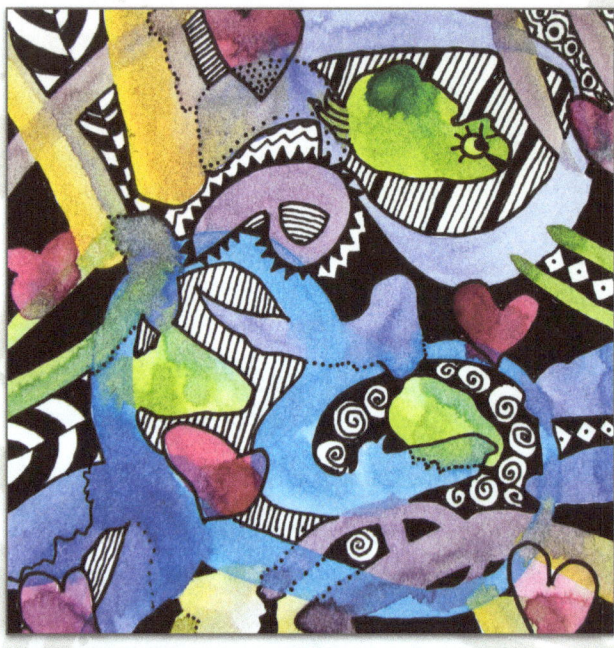
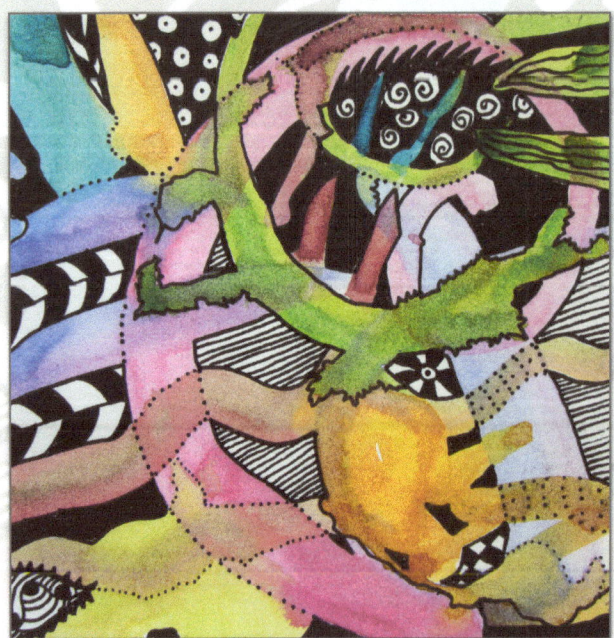
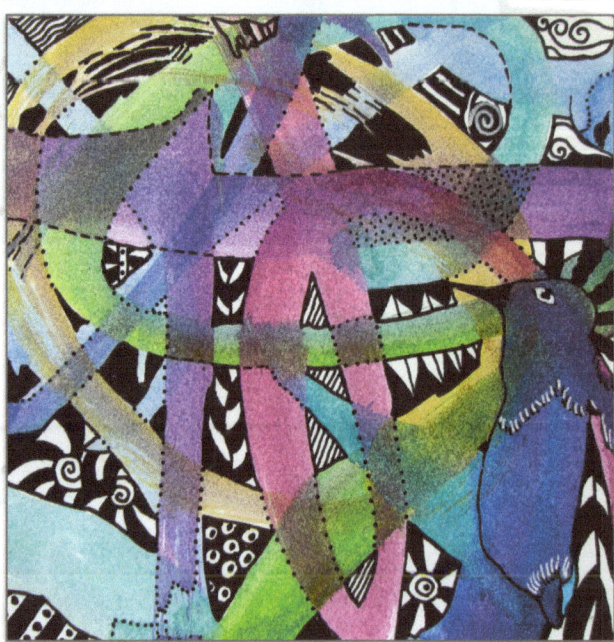

Smooth papers, card stock and boards work best for achieving crisp, fine lines.

DO YOU SEE WHAT I SEE?

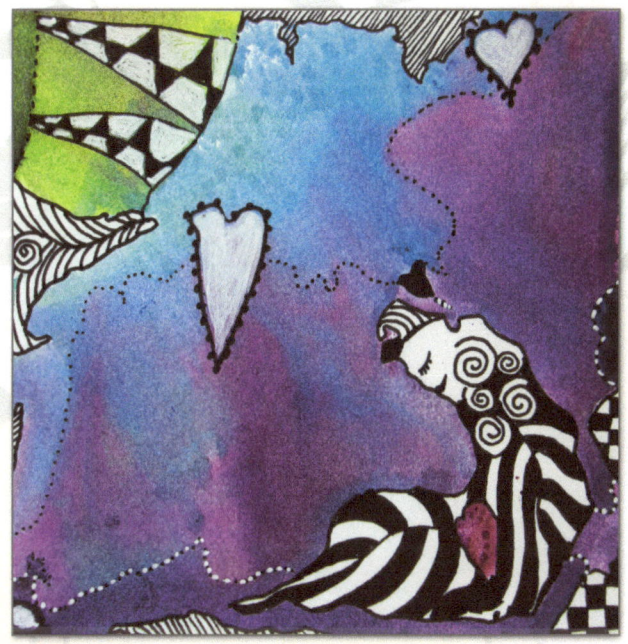
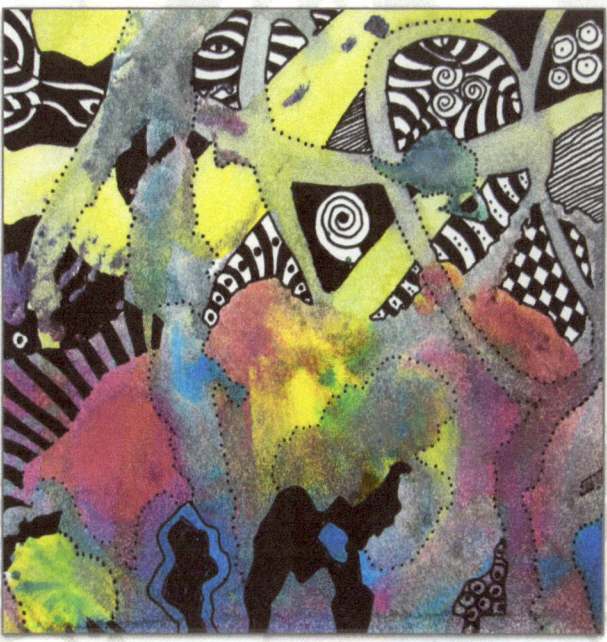
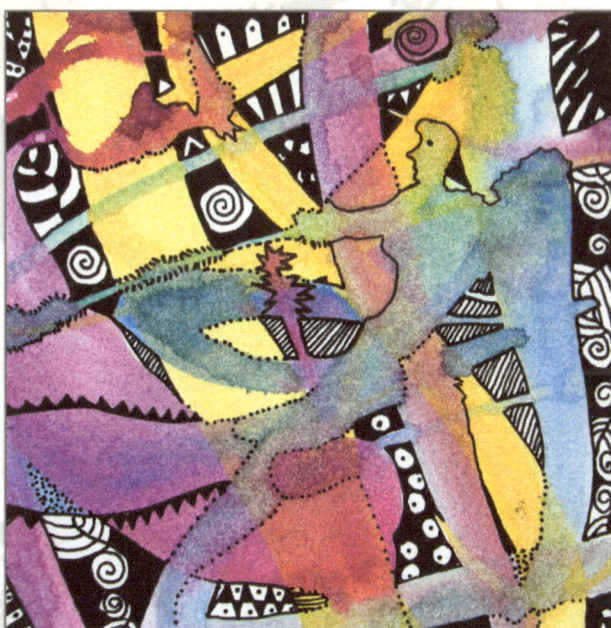
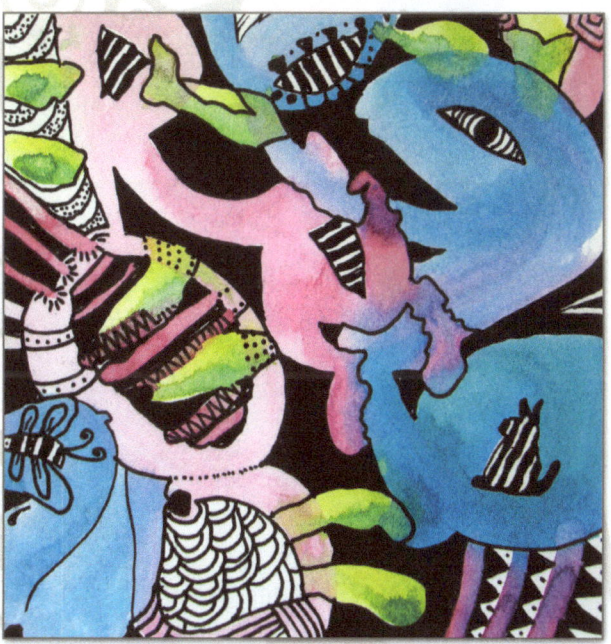

I see hearts, faces, insects, plant life, animals and sea creatures.

KUMOMI ON MASONITE

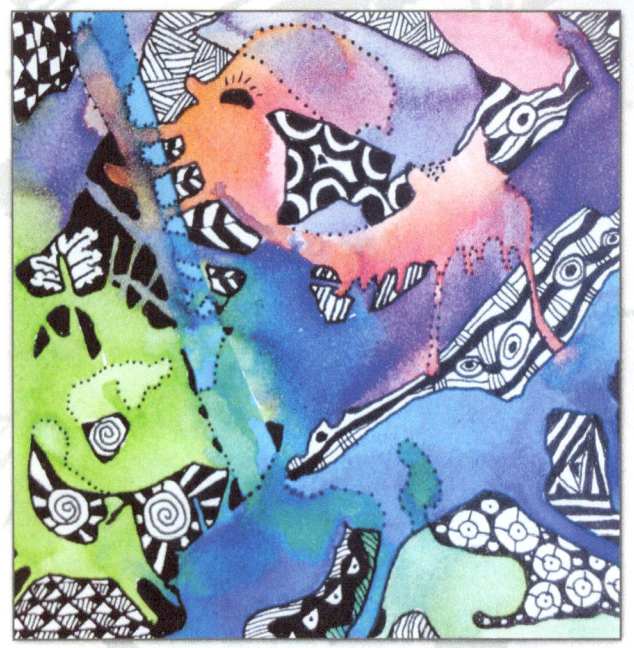 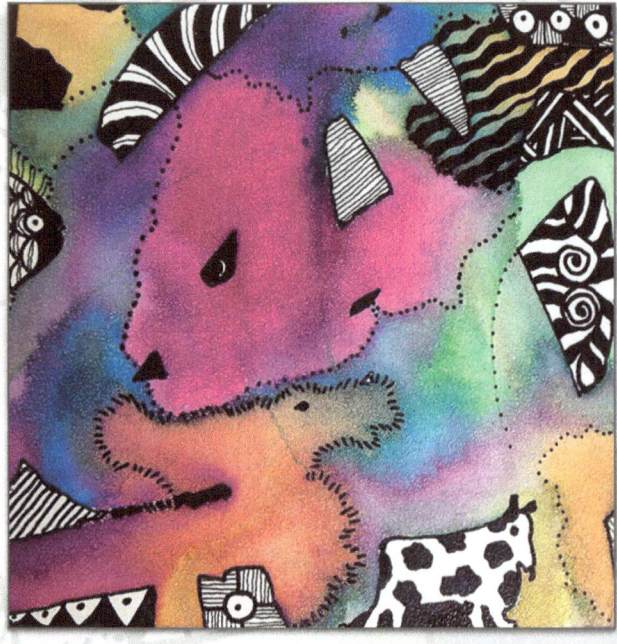

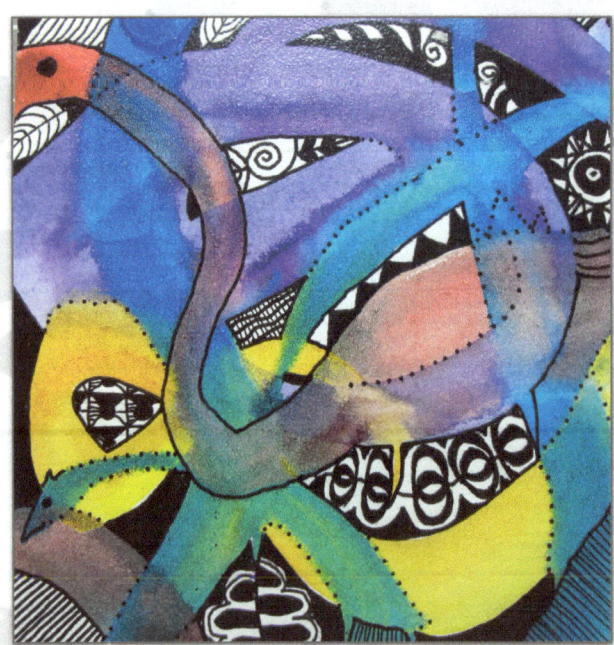 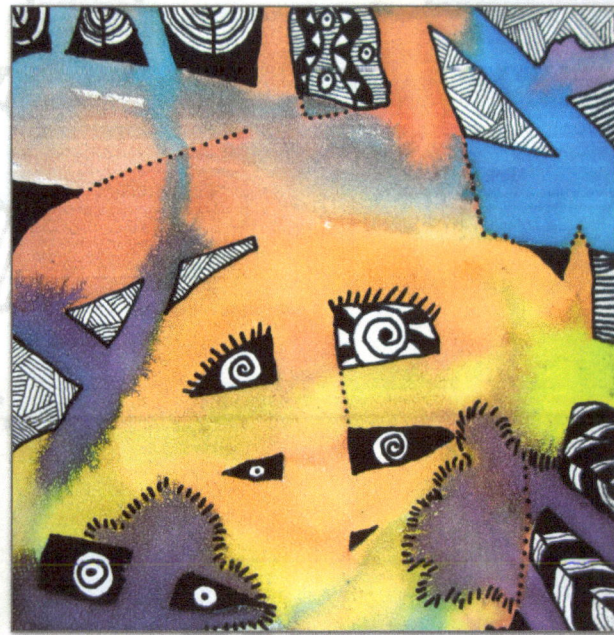

Masonite treated with white gesso is a great surface for Kumomi.

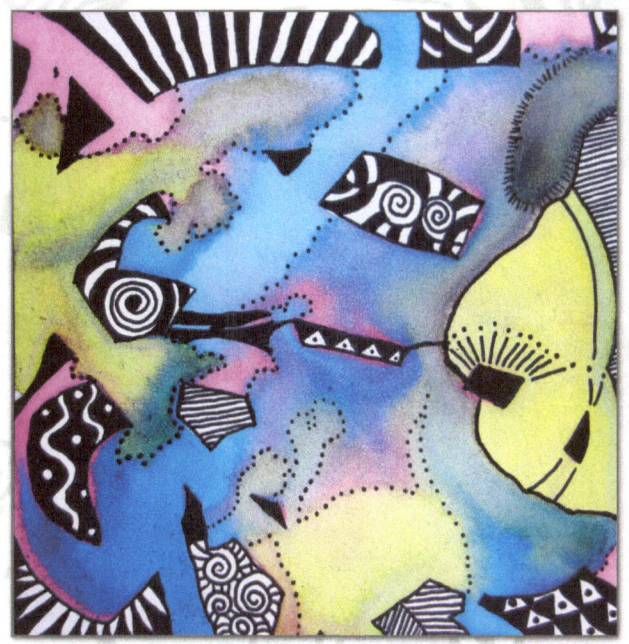 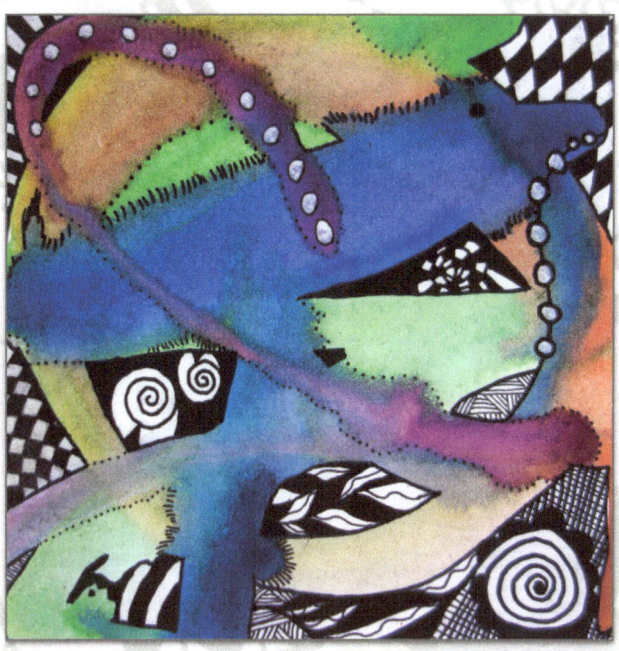

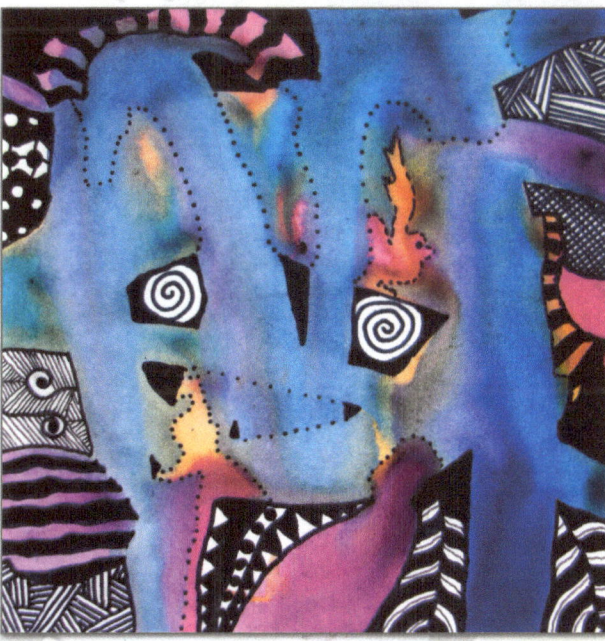 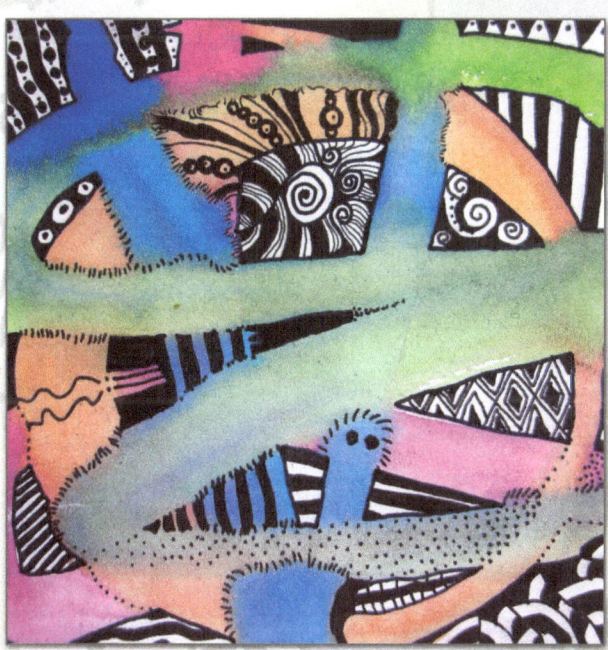

To make your own tiles, cut tempered masonite into 4″ squares, then apply a coat of gesso.

KUMOMI FOR KIDS

Many of the motions involved in Kumomi, such as holding a brush and drawing with a pen will help develop fine motor skills for children as young as five.

Practicing Kumomi will most likely help increase the ability to solve problems, enhance visual learning, inventiveness, concentration and communication skills and at the same time, increasing a sense of relaxation, self esteem and well being.

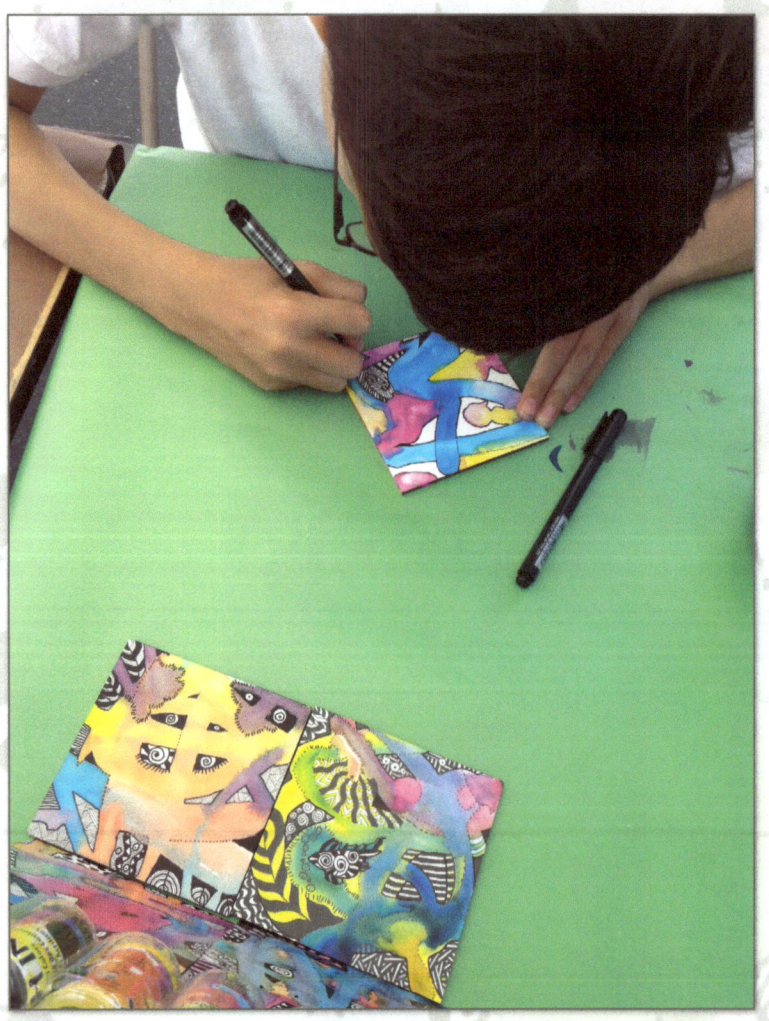
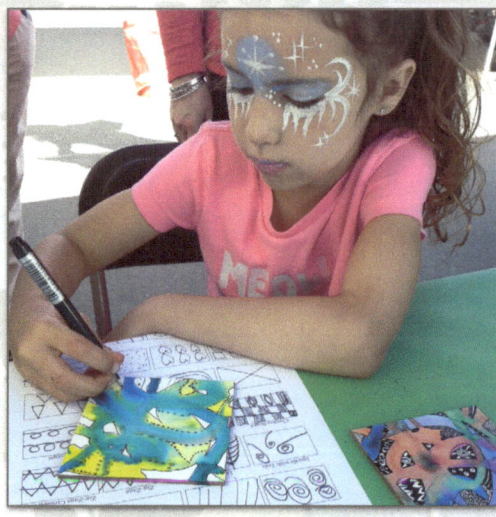
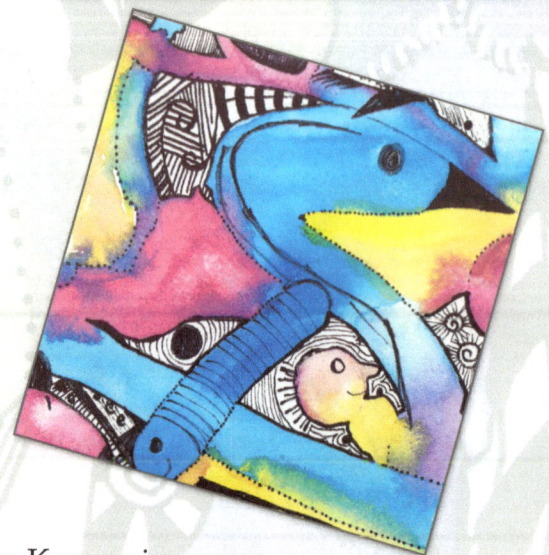

Children naturally enjoy the creative Kumomi process.

KUMOMI BY KIDS

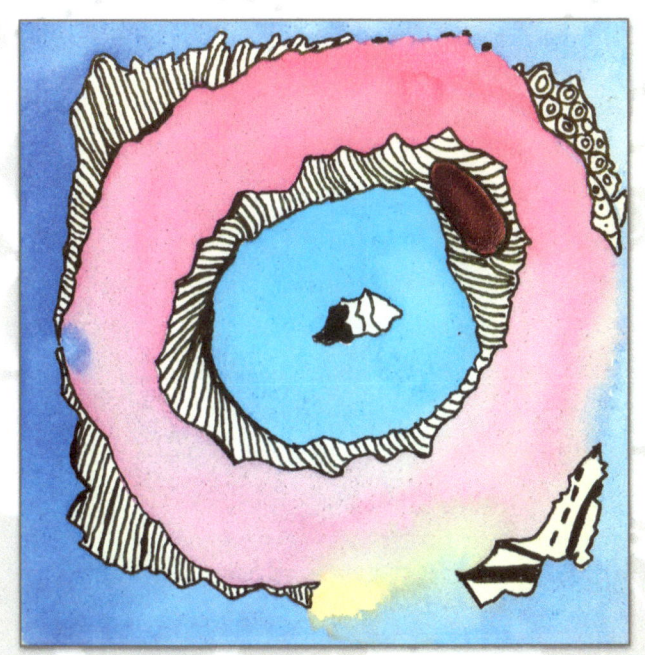
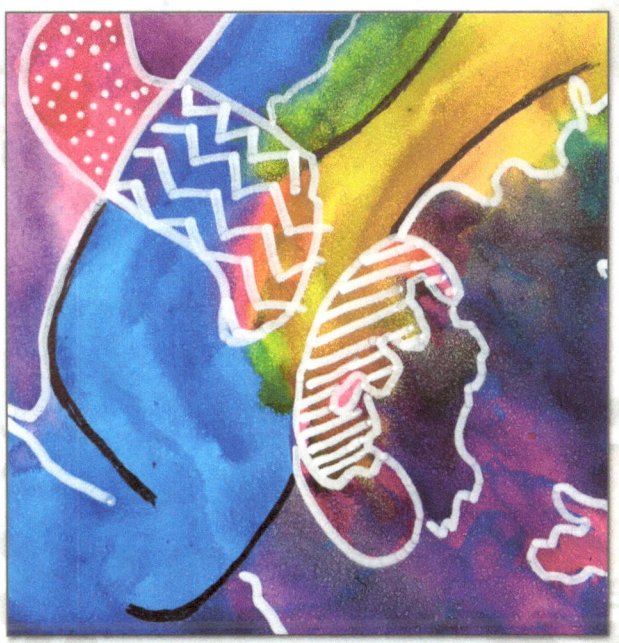
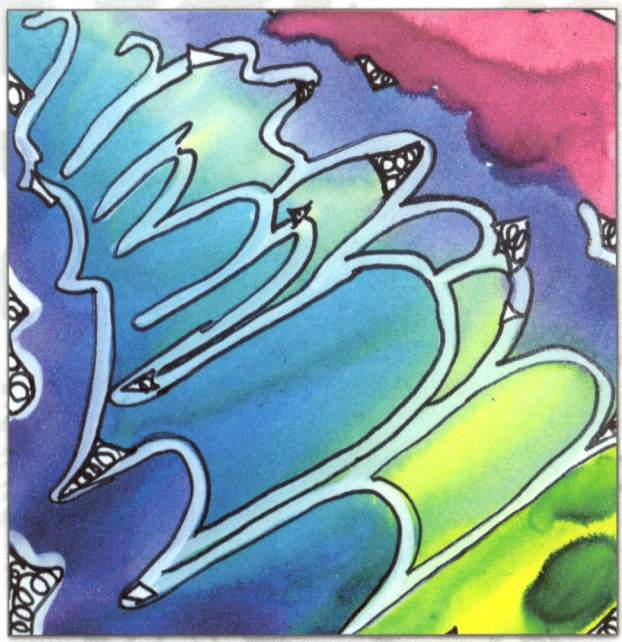
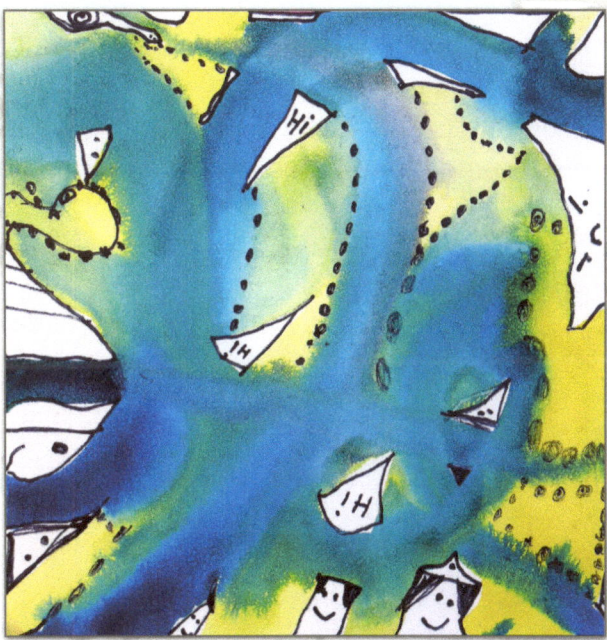

IDEAS & TIPS

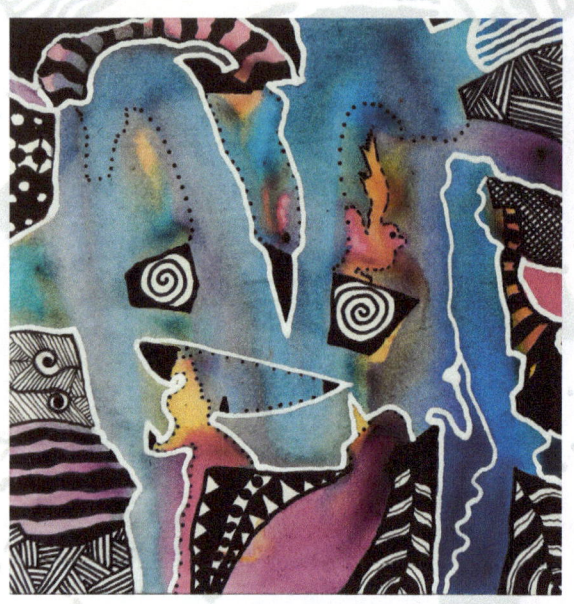

White pigmented opaque pens, paint markers and glitter pens can be used to bring out highlights if a painted area becomes too dark or if there isn't enough white left on the tile after you have painted it.

In the example on the left, I used a white opaque pen to brighten a dark tile which gave it more life. The opaque pens need to be waterproof so they don't rub off if you decide to varnish the tile later.

To make the finished tiles more durable, seal with an acrylic medium or varnish. Brush on several light coats with a soft, synthetic wide brush for a super smooth finish.

SPONTANEOUS PAINTING SUGGESTIONS

- Start with a soft round damp brush and use water generously while painting. Water helps move the colors on the tile and makes for interesting patterns and shapes.

- Clean your brush frequently in-between colors to keep them fresh and vibrant.

- Paint an area first with clear water and brush colors into the wet areas. Observe how the colors dance on the paper.

- Try picking up different colors with a small damp sponge and blot in random areas onto a tile. Watch the colors blend into the wet areas.

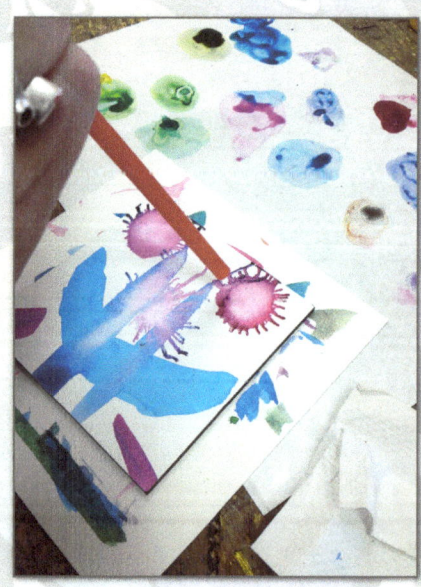

Use a plastic straw to make interesting effects by blowing gently into the wet areas of the paint.

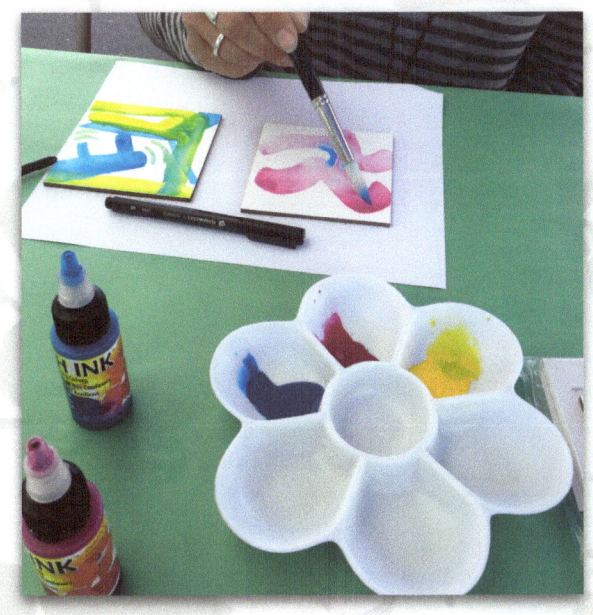

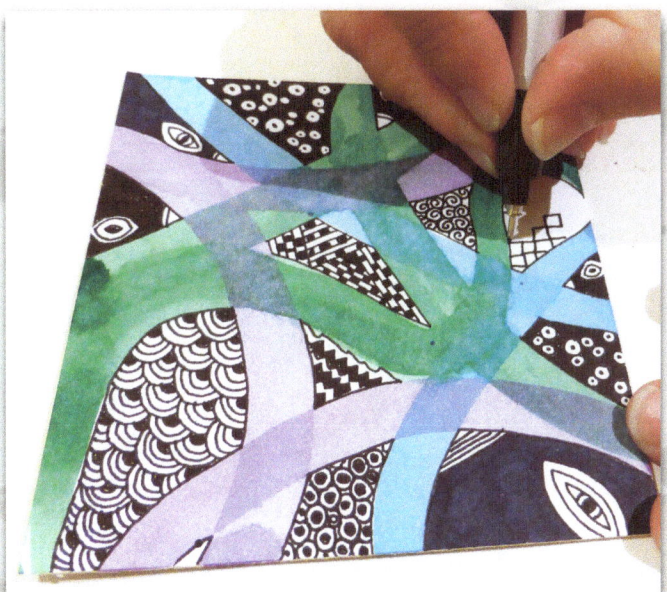

Lisa Lee

Ceramic or plastic palettes with divided sections are convenient and will allow you to mix and store a variety of colors when painting several tiles in one session. Wax paper and aluminum foil can be used as a palette and disposable palette paper pads are great to use when traveling.

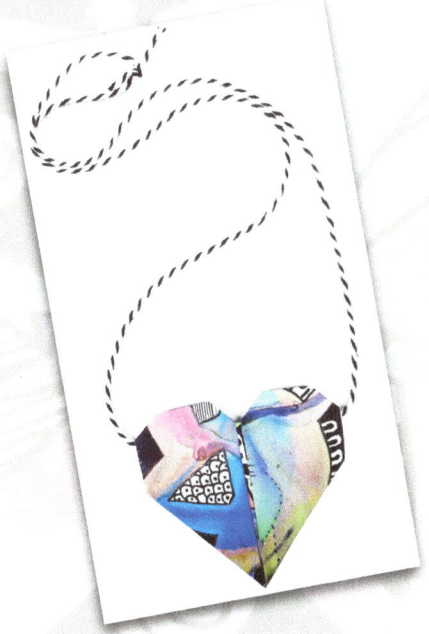

Kumomi Everywhere!

Kumomi can be done on almost anything that will accept paints and pens. Don't limit yourself to a square and give it a try on a smooth river rock or create a Kumomi journal and fill the pages with your meditations.

In this example I painted a sheet of white mineral origami paper with random colors then folded the heart. The patterns were drawn with a permanent fine tipped marker and the colors and ink did not smudge during the folding process.

Information on instructions for the heart necklace and mineral paper can be found in the resource section of this little book.

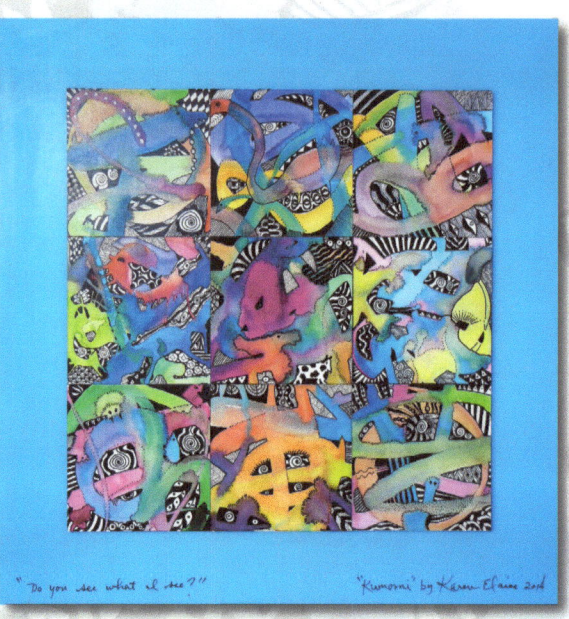

"Do you see what I see?"   'Kumomi' by Karen Elaine 2006

Masonite tiles can be made into functional objects such as boxes, trays or coasters. A great way to display finished tiles is to arrange several onto a larger painted piece of masonite or artist panel and hang on a wall.

In this example the panel was painted with light blue acrylic paint. White glue was applied on the backs of the tiles and secured to the front of the panel.

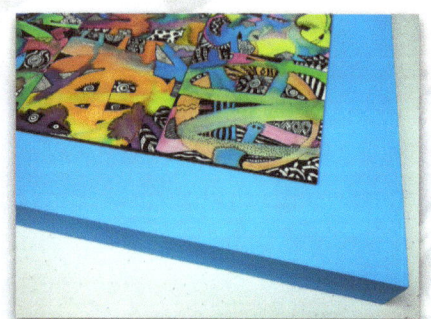

Brush some black acrylic paint on the edges of the tiles to make them look more finished.

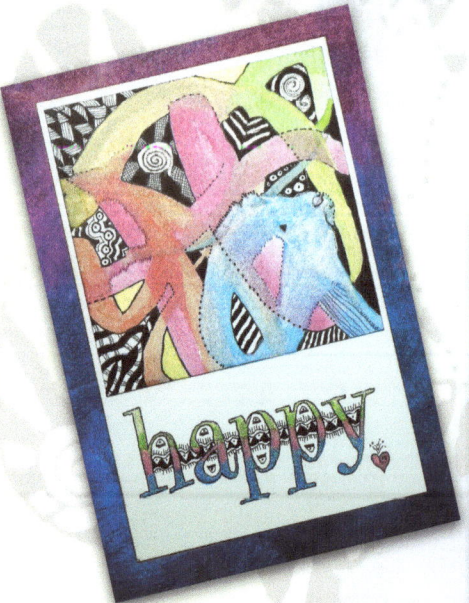

Highlight areas of the word with metallic paints or metallic pens.

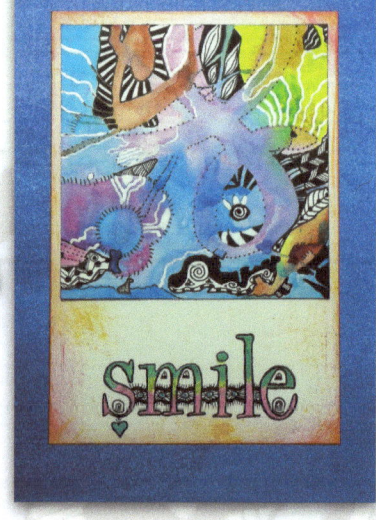

GREETING CARD IDEA

Stamp or write a word onto a blank piece of card stock and mindfully draw around the word.

 Assemble a finished Kumomi tile and the card with the word on a blank greeting card using glue or double stick adhesive. The blank greeting card in these examples were decorated with acrylic paint applied with a sponge.

STUDENT EXAMPLES

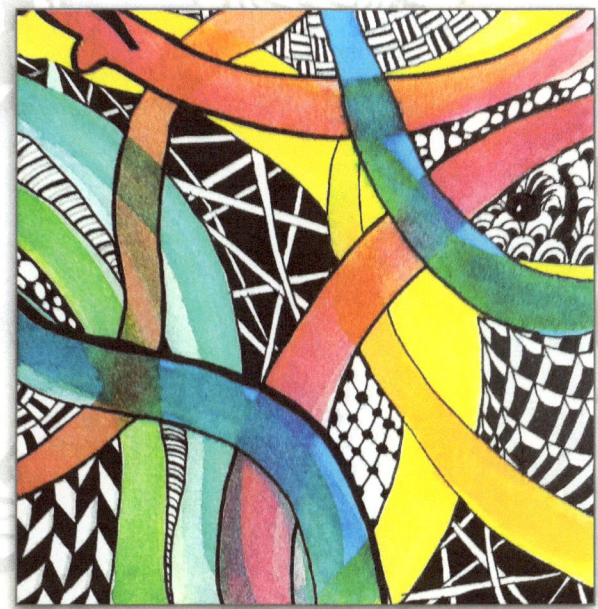

Melanie Fagerberg

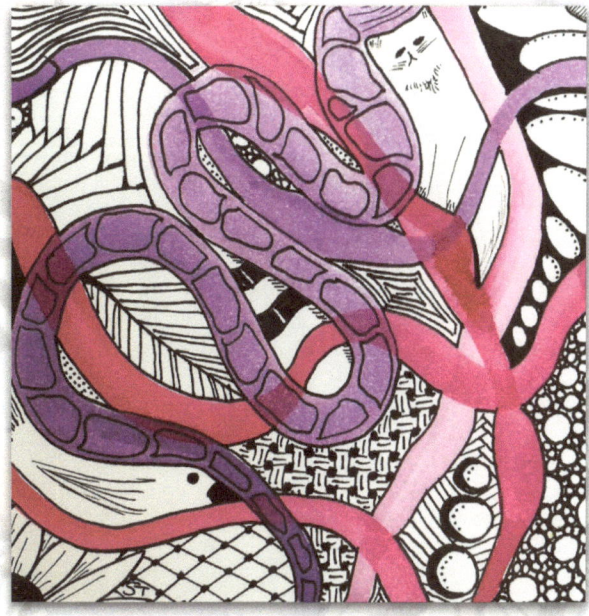

Sue Tipple

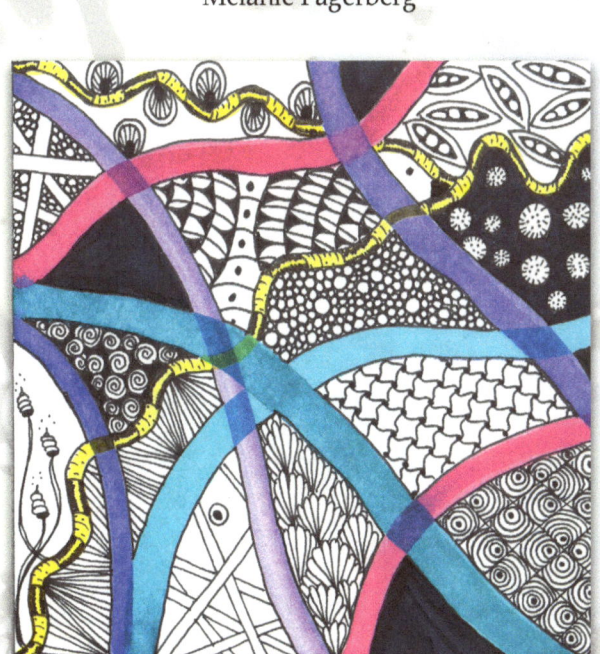

Dianne Johnson

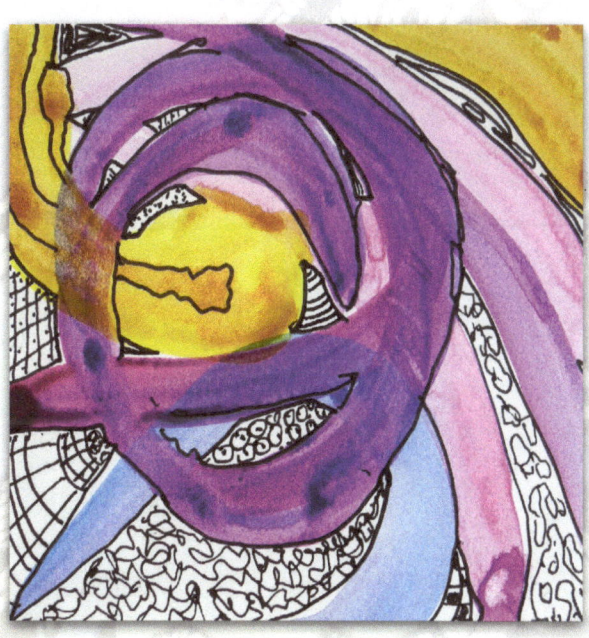

CAEA Student

KUMOMI FOR THE FIRST TIME

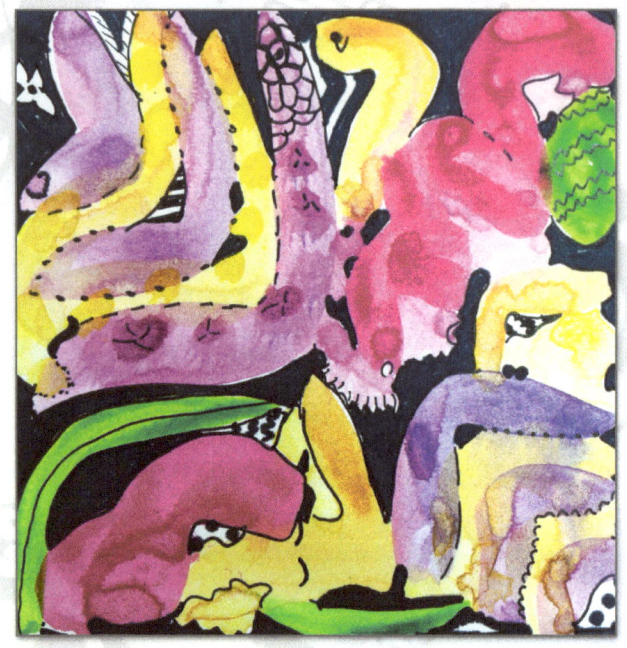
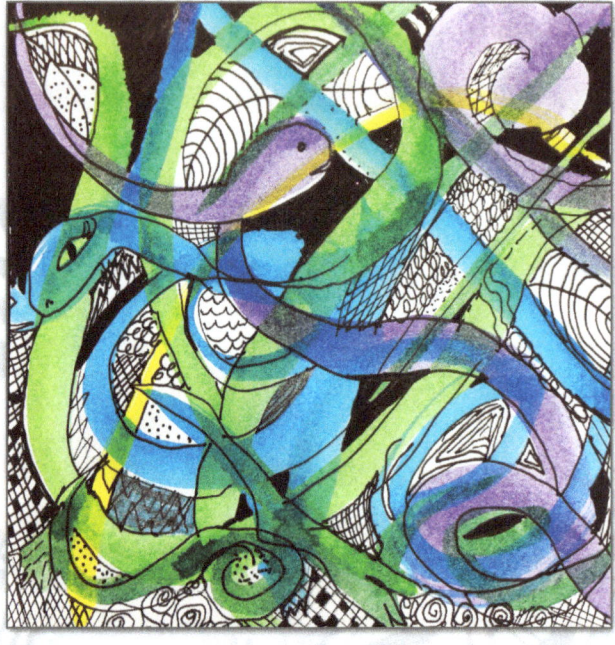
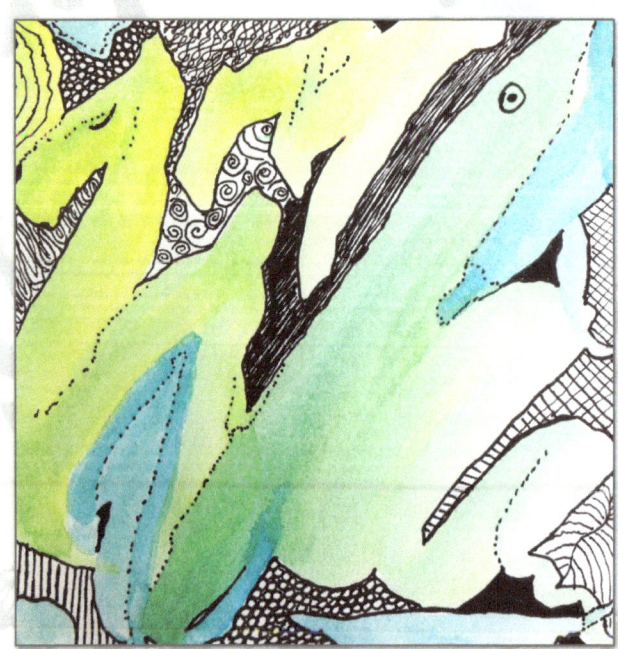
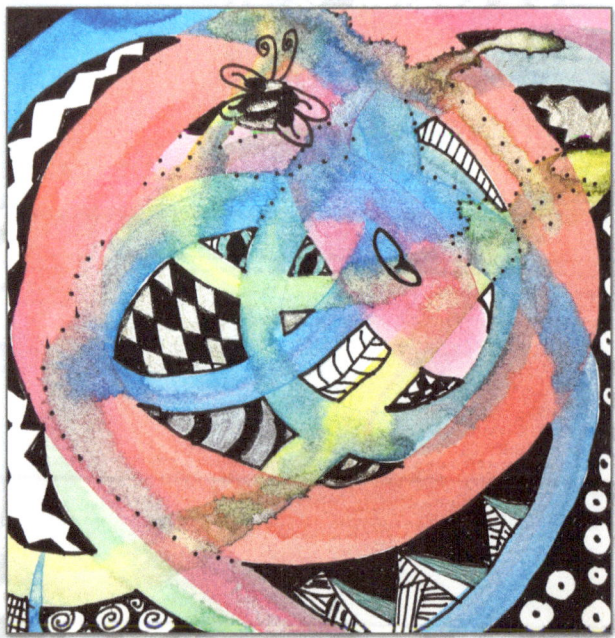

Examples of student work after their first Kumomi session.

RESOURCES

This is a list of suggested products that work best for me when I practice and teach Kumomi. Allow yourself to explore other products and supplies you have on hand as they will likely help you achieve the same goal of meditation, relaxation and increased creativity.

SPLASH INK, PERMAWRITER PENS, MINERAL PAPER & ORIGAMI HEART INSTRUCTIONS

Yasutomo Inc.
Burlingame, CA 94010
www.yasutomo.com

BRISTOL ARTIST TILES & PALETTE PAPER

Strathmore Artist Papers
Nenah, WI 54956
www.strathmoreartist.com

ART SQUARES

Inchie Arts LLC.
www.inchiearts.com

GESSOBORD ART PANELS 4"

Ampersand Art Supply
Buda, TX 78610
www.ampersandart.com

MICRON PENS, SOUFFLE OPAQUE PENS

Sakura of America
Hayward, CA, 94544
www.sakuraofamerica.com

MULTILINER PENS

Imagination International Inc.
Eugene, OR 97475
www.copicmarker.com

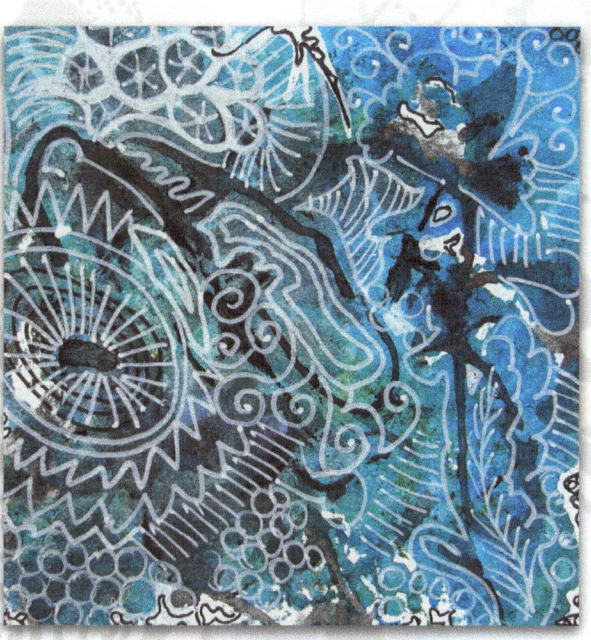

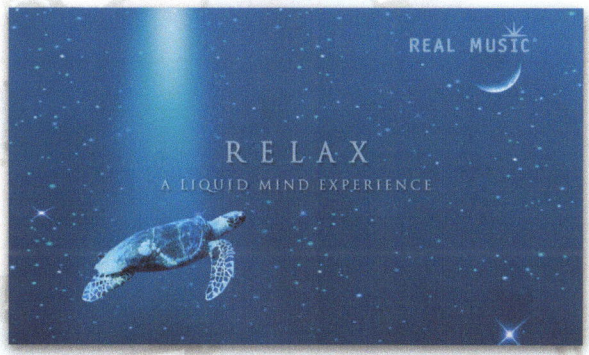

LIQUID MIND MUSIC ®

Available at iTunes, Amazon and streaming on Pandora radio.
www.liquidmindmusic.com

ABOUT THE AUTHOR

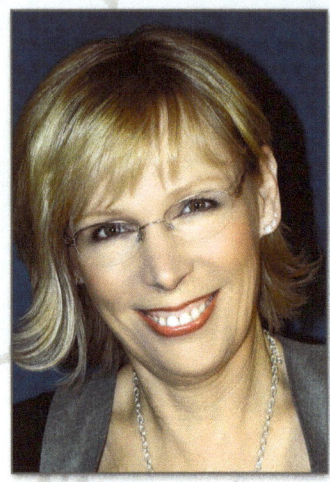

Karen Elaine is an artist, author and designer widely known as Karen Elaine Thomas. She combines her experience as a fine artist with her passion for paper to create unique and distinctive creative techniques. Karen developed Splash Ink, a simple color mixing system in which an infinite amount of colors can be created using only four basic colors.

She is the author of *Origami Card Craft, Mingei Crafts* and *Mizuhiki Magic* and is a featured artist in paper crafting books, magazines and DVD's

Karen developed the Kumomi creative process to enhance health and well being for herself, friends and family and is enjoying sharing the experience with others.

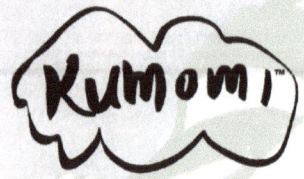

For more information, visit: www.karenelaine.com

www.ingramcontent.com/pod-product-compliance
Lightning Source LLC
Chambersburg PA
CBHW050424180526
45159CB00005B/2399